Original title:
Secrets in Shadows

Copyright © 2024 Creative Arts Management OÜ
All rights reserved.

Author: Adeline Fairfax
ISBN HARDBACK: 978-9916-90-318-6
ISBN PAPERBACK: 978-9916-90-319-3

Fragments of a Veiled Past

Whispers of time, soft and discreet,
Shadows of dreams lie at our feet.
Memories flicker like a distant flame,
Chasing the echoes, we play a game.

Pictures unfurl in the depths of the mind,
Faces once loved, now left behind.
Through broken glass, we seek the light,
Fragments of whispers melt into night.

Secrets Beneath the Skin

Every heartbeat hides a tale,
Underneath the flesh, there's a veil.
Silent stories linger and weave,
Promises made, yet hard to believe.

Tattoos of sorrow, inked in despair,
Map the emotions we choose not to share.
In the depths of our essence, truth must find,
The sacred secrets beneath the skin.

The Weight of Unsaid Words

Bottled feelings, deep and vast,
Words unspoken, shadows cast.
Each silence echoes like a bell,
Holding secrets we dare not tell.

The heart is heavy with all it keeps,
In quiet corners, the silence creeps.
Yet in the stillness, hope may stir,
To bridge the gap, a soft whisper.

In the Quiet of the Night

Stars are whispers in the sky,
In the stillness, dreams can fly.
Moonlight dances on the sea,
Casting shadows, setting thoughts free.

Nighttime cradles every sigh,
Holds the secrets we can't deny.
In this place, hearts truly see,
What it means to simply be.

Hushed Reflections

In the stillness of night,
Whispers trace the air,
Shadows dance in moonlight,
Dreams linger with care.

Glimmers of hopes fade,
Thoughts drift like soft sighs,
In this quiet cascade,
Truth floats, never lies.

Moments lost in time,
Memories softly fade,
In silence, they chime,
A gentle serenade.

As dawn greets the sky,
The echoes depart,
Yet in every goodbye,
There's a piece of the heart.

Ghosts of the Unsaid

In the corners of mind,
Secrets softly dwell,
Voices left behind,
In a muted shell.

Words that never came,
Haunt the restless night,
Each an untamed flame,
Flickering in the light.

Stories left untold,
In silence, they weave,
Threads of the bold,
In dreams, they believe.

Yet, in shadows' dance,
Fear begins to fade,
With each forgotten chance,
A new truth is made.

The Veil of Darkness

Underneath the stars,
Mysteries entwine,
Veils conceal the scars,
Of moments divine.

Shadows cloak my fears,
Whispers touch the soul,
Through the mist of years,
I strive to be whole.

Each step in this gloom,
Guides me through the night,
As whispers consume,
The wish for the light.

Yet hope starts to gleam,
In the quiet air,
Beneath the dream's seam,
A spark shines with care.

Tread Softly Through the Veils

Tread softly, my friend,
Through ebon-hued night,
Where dreams twist and bend,
And shadows take flight.

A world wrapped in hue,
Of twilight's embrace,
Each step we pursue,
Leaves a delicate trace.

Through whispers and sighs,
In the dark, we roam,
Searching for the wise,
To guide us back home.

In the heart of the veils,
Where silence is loud,
Let the light fill our sails,
And lift us, unbowed.

Unraveled Threads

Once woven tight, now frayed and bare,
Echoes of laughter hang in the air.
Colors of memories fade and blend,
A tapestry lost, where dreams descend.

Fingers trace paths on a broken seam,
Whispers of hope in a distant dream.
Each strand a story, a role to play,
In the fabric of life, we drift away.

The knots we tied are now loose and worn,
In the silence, softly we mourn.
Yet still the heart beats, resilience shown,
Among all the threads, we are not alone.

In the chaos, beauty finds its way,
Through unraveled threads, we learn to sway.
A new design forms in the gentle light,
From frayed beginnings, we take our flight.

The Cryptic Embrace

In shadows deep, secrets entwined,
A touch so soft, yet hard to find.
Promises linger in the midnight air,
A cryptic embrace, two souls laid bare.

Beneath the moonlight, stories unfold,
Words left unspoken, mysteries told.
With every heartbeat, tension ignites,
In silence we linger, amidst starry nights.

Glimmers of hope in timeless dance,
Caught in a spell, a fleeting glance.
Each whisper a melody, ethereal grace,
In the cryptic night, we find our place.

As dawn breaks softly, we'll part our ways,
Yet in heart's corners, love's echo plays.
A bond sealed tight, with a secret trace,
Forever we'll cherish, this cryptic embrace.

Beneath the Surface

Ripples spread wide in a tranquil sea,
Beneath the calm, hidden depths foresee.
Echoes of whispers in water's caress,
Secrets submerged, in silence they press.

Shells hold the stories of ages gone by,
Scratches of time beneath azure sky.
Silent confessions that fish cannot hear,
Beneath the surface, truth's held near.

Coral turns vibrant with life intertwined,
A dance of existence, so perfectly timed.
Yet shadows may linger where light rarely leads,
Beneath the surface, the ocean still bleeds.

So dive a bit deeper, embrace the unknown,
For treasures await where the currents have blown.
Life's tapestry woven through layers of grace,
Awaits all who wander beneath the surface.

Twilight's Hidden Stories

As daylight wanes, whispers arise,
In twilight's glow, the world softly sighs.
Shadows stretch long, embracing the night,
Hidden stories stir, just out of sight.

Each star a witness, a tale to unfold,
In the quietude, mysteries bold.
Dreamers awaken to visions so clear,
Twilight reveals what the heart holds dear.

The breeze carries laughter, a soft serenade,
While secrets emerge from the dusk's cool shade.
Flickering lanterns guide paths once lost,
In twilight's embrace, we bear the cost.

Let the stories weave through heart and mind,
As the veil of night beckons us to find.
In each fleeting moment, a life's true glory,
We linger in twilight, where hidden stories.

Labyrinth of the Dark

In shadows deep where whispers creep,
The paths entwine, the secrets keep.
A flicker dim, the silence moans,
Forgotten trails, the heart bemoans.

Through twisted ways, the echoes call,
A presence felt, yet naught at all.
The maze of fear, it pulls me near,
To face the night, to find what's dear.

With every turn, a silence grows,
The heartbeat races, the tension flows.
A lantern's glow, a guiding spark,
A way to light the labyrinth dark.

Yet hope persists within the gloom,
To find a path, to break the doom.
The dark may weave its intricate lace,
But in its heart, I'll find my place.

Silence Sings

In twilight's hush, where shadows lie,
The silence sings a soft goodbye.
Each note a breath, each pause a dream,
An echo felt, yet never seen.

The stars awake, their whispers bright,
In moonlit folds, the stillness bites.
A lullaby for weary souls,
In quiet realms, the heart consoles.

Through gentle night, the songbirds soar,
Their melodies, a distant roar.
In every heartbeat, every wing,
The world transforms as silence sings.

So close your eyes and lend an ear,
Let silence wrap you, hold you near.
Within its arms, the peace will bring,
A wondrous calm where silence sings.

Shadows That Speak

In the quiet of night, they glide,
Casting tales where secrets hide.
Whispers soft as the autumn breeze,
Drawing close with a silent tease.

Through the moonlight, they take form,
Bending light, a gentle storm.
Voices mingling in the dark,
Where shadows dance and leave their mark.

Lost in time, they float and sway,
Guiding hearts that lose their way.
Every movement tells a truth,
Echoes of their ancient youth.

In the corners where dreams converge,
The shadows stir, they start to surge.
Listening closely, you will find,
The stories etched in every mind.

Whispers of the Unknown

Underneath the starlit sky,
Mysteries whisper, low and sly.
Each sound a secret, soft and clear,
A call from worlds that linger near.

In the folds of the moonlit night,
Hidden truths begin to ignite.
Voices wander, seeking light,
Drawing wanderers to their plight.

Through the forest, shadows weave,
With tales that the night may conceive.
Every rustle hints at fate,
In silence, destinies await.

With every breath, the dark unfolds,
As gentle secrets, life upholds.
Listen close, the unknown sings,
Lost in wonder, the heart takes wings.

Veils of Twilight

As daylight fades, shadows descend,
Wrapped in whispers, the night extends.
Veils of twilight, soft and light,
Cradle dreams that take their flight.

Colors blend in the dusky hue,
Painting skies with a tranquil view.
Every moment drips with grace,
Time slows down in this sacred space.

In the hush of the evening glow,
Mysteries rise, like seeds to sow.
As stars appear, the world turns slow,
Veils of twilight, a gentle show.

Held in silence, the heart takes pause,
In this magic, we find our cause.
Every sigh, a sweet refrain,
In twilight's arms, we feel no pain.

Hidden Echoes

In the stillness, echoes play,
Dancing softly, fading away.
Unseen whispers fill the air,
Secrets linger everywhere.

Through the halls of memory's keep,
Stories echo, secrets seep.
Each heartbeat, a lesson learned,
In the silence, the spirit yearned.

Beneath the surface, currents flow,
Tales of old that gently glow.
With every glance, they reappear,
Hidden echoes, crisp and clear.

In the depths of the restless night,
Lost voices sing beneath the light.
Listen closely, let them in,
For hidden echoes always begin.

The Art of Quietude

In stillness, the whispers hide,
Amid the shadows, they abide.
A moment's peace, a breath so light,
The world stands still, draped in night.

Soft echoes dance on velvet air,
An ancient song, a silent prayer.
Hushed tones weave in twilight's loom,
Cradle the heart in gentle bloom.

Nature breathes, a soft caress,
In solitude, we find our rest.
Each pause a canvas framed in grace,
In quietude, we find our place.

Beneath the stars, a sacred bond,
In silence, we learn to respond.
The art of quiet, pure and true,
Reveals the soul, its vibrant hue.

Muffled Secrets

Whispers linger in the air,
Soft confessions, light as hair.
Shadows cloak what we conceal,
Muffled truths, a silent reel.

Beneath the surface, currents flow,
Unseen stories we may not show.
In quiet corners, dreams collide,
Guarded moments, worlds abide.

Veiled intentions, eyes that speak,
In the hush, it's hope we seek.
Remembered laughter, stolen sighs,
In tangled thoughts, the heart replies.

Each muted sound, a gem so bright,
Found in the depths of endless night.
Muffled secrets softly dwell,
In every heart, a hidden spell.

Secrets Beneath the Canopy

The trees weave tales of days long past,
In dappled light, shadows are cast.
Leaves whisper low, secrets unfurl,
Nature's book in a silent whirl.

Roots intertwine beneath the ground,
Hushed stories in silence bound.
In emerald threads, life intertwines,
Ancient whispers, hidden signs.

Mossy carpets cradle the floor,
Each step reveals an open door.
The air, thick with scents divine,
Beneath the boughs, dreams entwine.

Sunlit patches, where secrets gleam,
In canopies, we chase our dream.
Nature's heart beats slow and true,
Within its depths, a world anew.

The Lurking Unknown

In shadows deep, where silence reigns,
Lurks the unknown, breaking chains.
A heartbeat skips, the air feels thick,
Mysteries wane in darkness, quick.

The night unfolds its heavy shroud,
In corners dark, fears gather loud.
Eyes unseen, watch with intent,
A chilling breeze, time's lament.

The path ahead is veiled in shade,
What lies beyond, a choice we've made.
In every rustle, secrets quake,
In the unknown, we feel awake.

Yet through the fear, we dare to tread,
With hopes alight, we forge ahead.
Embrace the darkness, shadows shown,
For in the night, we find our own.

Under the Cover of Dusk

Whispers float in twilight's breath,
Shadows shift with silent grace,
Stars awaken from their rest,
Moonlight paints a silver trace.

Branches sway with gentle ease,
Crickets sing their evening song,
Night wraps earth in velvet peace,
Time slips by, it won't be long.

Footsteps echo on the street,
Softened by the dimming light,
Hearts and dreams in shadows meet,
Secrets stir within the night.

Calm descends as day takes flight,
Colors fade to shades of grey,
In the quiet, find your sight,
Under dusk, the lost will stay.

Encrypted in the Half-Light

Words unspoken, wrapped in fear,
Murmurs linger through the gloom,
Truths lie buried, drawing near,
Secrets find a shaded room.

Flickering flames of doubt arise,
Figures dance in shades of dark,
Every glance holds veiled goodbyes,
Hidden truths leave only sparks.

Time is caught in muted flow,
Hesitations weigh the air,
Half-light hides what we can't show,
Glances traded, moments rare.

Decrypt the silence, feel the pull,
Between the shadows, worlds collide,
In the half-light, voices lull,
Whispers echo, secrets bide.

Sotto Voce in the Gloom

Silent sighs slip through the night,
Muffled thoughts in velvet dark,
Voices low, yet filled with light,
In the shadows, kindled spark.

Breathless moments hold their breath,
Softly weaving tales untold,
In the hush, we flirt with death,
Whispers warm against the cold.

Echoes linger by the glass,
Time distorts, the mind's retreat,
Words that flicker, ghostly pass,
Sotto voce, hearts must meet.

In the gloom, we dare to dream,
Underneath the weight of stars,
Life unfolds like hidden themes,
In soft tones, we chase our scars.

Tendrils of the Unspoken

Fingers trace the air between,
Words that linger, yet unsaid,
In the quiet, visions glean,
Thoughts entwined where silence led.

Vines of doubt twist in the mind,
Every glance a thread unspooled,
Tendrils reach, the heart confined,
In the silence, truth is ruled.

Moments stretch like shadows cast,
Fleeting glances, stolen breath,
Grasping at what's meant to last,
In this stillness, there is death.

Echoes weave through tangled lanes,
Lost in labyrinths of the heart,
Tendrils pull with gentle strains,
Whispers soft, they play their part.

Submerged Murmurs

Whispers of the deep call,
In shadows, secrets weave and crawl.
Bubbles rise like thoughts unspoken,
In silence, ancient bonds are broken.

Echoes dance in twilight's gloom,
Softly swaying, lost in bloom.
Currents tug at dreams half-glimpsed,
In stillness, knowledge, forever nursed.

Ripples shimmer, stories told,
Tales of heart, both fierce and bold.
Below the waves, where hopes do sail,
The ocean breathes, a siren's tale.

In depths where sunlight falters,
The pulse of time, the heart that alters.
Each murmur finds a place to rest,
In the embrace of waters blessed.

The Hidden Pathway

Amongst the trees, a trail discreet,
Whispers linger where shadows meet.
Soft moss carpets the winding way,
Guiding footsteps where spirits play.

Sunlight dapples through leaves above,
A secret path, a gentle shove.
Each turn reveals a world anew,
Where hopes take flight and dreams pursue.

Vines entwine, a living gate,
Nature's bounty, love and fate.
Follow the signs, the subtle clues,
In this abyss, find your muse.

With every step, the heart beats strong,
The hidden path, where you belong.
Into the wild, be brave, be free,
Where the soul dances in harmony.

Riddles Beneath the Surface

Layers of thought, a tangled maze,
Questions linger, in a haze.
Beneath the calm, a storm does stir,
In silence, truth begins to blur.

Each pluck of string, a note concealed,\nRiddles murmur fate revealed.
What lies beneath the mirrored glass,
A glimpse of self, where shadows pass.

Fragments haunt, like whispers lost,
The price of knowing, the bitter cost.
In answers found, yet questions chime,
A timeless game, the dance of time.

Dig deeper still, through veils of fright,
Light and dark in eternal flight.
For every riddle that time bestows,
A truth awaits, that softly glows.

A Half-Formed Truth

In twilight's grasp, the shadows bend,
Whispers falter, truths transcend.
A fragile sense, like mist and air,
Half-formed echoes, everywhere.

Stories left on tongues unspent,
Promises broken, hearts still rent.
The light and dark, they intertwine,
In silence, thoughts refuse to shine.

Perceptions blurred by endless strife,
A tapestry of healing life.
What does it mean to find your way?
When every truth is led astray.

Yet in the chaos, hope will gleam,
A flicker of light, a distant dream.
Let the half-formed take their flight,
And weave the darkness into light.

Silhouettes of Whispered Thoughts

In shadows cast by fading light,
Dreams dance softly, taking flight.
Echoes linger, soft and low,
Silent secrets, hearts bestow.

Veils of silence, thoughts entwined,
In the quiet, truth we find.
Whispered tales of sun and moon,
Carry softly, destiny's tune.

Gentle breezes through the trees,
Carry whispers with such ease.
Silent sighs and tender calls,
Resonate within these walls.

Lost in wonder, moment's trance,
In the silence, thoughts advance.
Silhouettes of what could be,
Awakening the soul to free.

In the Embrace of Nightfall

Stars awaken in silent skies,
As the day softly dies.
Moonlight spills on sleeping ground,
In night's embrace, peace is found.

Whispers of the dusk surround,
Mysteries in shadows abound.
Veils of darkness gently fall,
Cradling dreams, a nightingale's call.

Stillness reigns, the world to rest,
In twilight's arms, we feel blessed.
Time suspended, breath held tight,
In the depth of soothing night.

With open hearts, we seek to roam,
In the embrace, we find our home.
Through muted tones and peaceful grace,
In the stillness, we find our place.

Veils of Forgotten Time

In the echoes of the past,
Memories fade, yet hold fast.
Veils of time, they softly weave,
Stories hidden, spirits cleave.

Ancient whispers, tales untold,
In the silence, truths unfold.
Fragments linger, softly known,
In the heartbeats, seeds are sown.

Silent shadows, glimmers of old,
In the softness, courage bold.
Veils of twilight, dimming light,
Guard the secrets of the night.

Journey back through history's tide,
In forgotten corners, dreams abide.
Embrace the echoes, let them shine,
In the tapestry of forgotten time.

Lingering Mysterious Mists

In the morning, mists arise,
Veiling nature's soft disguise.
Whispers curl in gentle sways,
Mysteries dance through dawn's grey rays.

A tapestry of fog and dream,
Life flows softly, like a stream.
Lingering secrets in the air,
Nature's heart, so hidden, rare.

With each breath, enchantment grows,
Where the silent river flows.
Veils of mist, a gentle kiss,
In the stillness, moments bliss.

Embrace the magic, let it stay,
In the mists, we find our way.
Dancing softly, shadows play,
Lingering dreams at break of day.

Echoes in the Abyss

Whispers of shadows pass me by,
In the silence, secrets lie.
Faint reflections from the past,
Echoes linger, fading fast.

Darkened waters pull me near,
Drowning thoughts I cannot clear.
Voices carried on the tide,
Lost within, I try to hide.

Footsteps tread on hollow ground,
In this void, no hope is found.
A distant call, a beckoning,
From the depths, my heart starts sinking.

Yet within this vast expanse,
Resilience sparks a fleeting chance.
Between despair and light, I drift,
In the abyss, the soul will lift.

Confounding Curiosities

In the attic, dust-clad dreams,
Curiosities burst at the seams.
Forgotten toys and weathered hats,
Each a story among the chats.

Glimmers of time, a fading glance,
Mysteries wrapped in a silent dance.
Trinkets whisper, tales untold,
In their depths, the past unfolds.

Why do some treasures catch the eye?
What draws the heart, and why, oh why?
Layers of wonder, peeling away,
Curiosities lead us astray.

Seeking answers in things obscure,
In the strange, we find what's pure.
Every question stirs the mind,
A journey rich with truths to find.

The Muted Symphony

In shadows cast by fading light,
A silence falls, the world feels tight.
Notes unplayed, a breath held long,
The muted symphony feels wrong.

In every room, a silent tune,
Faint echoes rise, a distant moon.
Melodies linger, longing for air,
But silence reigns, a heavy care.

What happened to the vibrant sound?
Where did the joy of music drown?
In whispered dreams, the rhythm sleeps,
Yet in our hearts, the longing creeps.

With hopes to break the deafening hush,
We seek the notes in the wild rush.
A symphony waits, concealed in shade,
Ready to play, the silence frayed.

Glimpses of the Unseen

In the corner of my weary eye,
Fleeting shapes begin to fly.
Whispers hidden in the breeze,
Glimpses come with such unease.

What wonders hide beyond our sight?
In shadows thick, there's strange delight.
A shimmer here, a shadow there,
Unseen realms, yet everywhere.

Voices echo from afar,
Calling out like a distant star.
In the quiet, secrets bloom,
Glimpses of the night's perfumed gloom.

As the dawn begins to break,
Revealing paths we long to take.
In every glance, the mysteries tease,
Glimpses of what lies beneath the trees.

Dances of the Invisible

In twilight's hush, shadows sway,
Echoes of dreams drift away.
Whispers of life, soft and bright,
Invisible waltzes greet the night.

The stars blink gently, a silent cue,
While phantoms of hope dance anew.
Silent music weaves through the air,
In this world, they dance without care.

Faint footsteps trace the midnight ground,
Where secrets lie deep, yet unbound.
A ballet of thoughts, unseen and free,
Carried by winds, they long to be.

In the end, as dawn breaks clear,
The dances fade, but linger near.
For in every heartbeat, a story lives,
Of the invisible dance that time gives.

The Deep Cradle of Enigma

In shadows cast by the candle's glow,
Mysteries whisper, soft and slow.
Each riddle wrapped in gentle night,
A puzzle beckons, hidden from sight.

Echoes of thoughts drift through the dark,
The spark of wonder ignites a mark.
Circles of fate draw near to close,
In the cradle where silence grows.

Deep waters cradle secrets untold,
Stories woven in threads of gold.
In every ripple, a tale to share,
The depths of enigma take us there.

Awake, awake! the mind shall see,
The profound dance of mystery.
In the cradle of night, soft and wide,
The heart finds truth where shadows abide.

Unwhispered

In the quiet hum of an empty room,
Words unspoken break the gloom.
Each breath a secret, held so tight,
Lost in the depths of black and white.

Eyes exchange what lips won't say,
In silence, meanings drift and sway.
A glance that lingers, heavy with weight,
Holds the promise of love or fate.

Moments freeze in fragile light,
Unwhispered hopes take flight,
In the tapestry of stillness spun,
A bond is forged, two become one.

Yet echoes of thoughts, hushed and meek,
Paint the canvas where hearts speak.
In the sacred silence, we come to know,
The beauty found in the unwhispered flow.

Secrets of the Moonlit Veil

Beneath the glow of the silver sphere,
Whispers of twilight draw us near.
Secrets dance on the edge of sight,
Wrapped in shadows of the night.

The moonbeams spill like a silken thread,
Guiding the lost where dreams are fed.
Softly, they weave the tales untold,
In a world where magic unfolds.

The trees sway gently, their secrets kept,
While the stars above quietly wept.
For in the stillness, hearts reveal
The whispers hidden in the moonlit veil.

Come, linger here in this sacred space,
Where time holds still in the night's embrace.
With every secret shared and given,
We find our truth, entwined and driven.

Lurking in the Half-light

In the dusk where whispers fade,
Shadows dance, a silent parade.
Secrets linger in the air,
Half-light shrouds what's hidden there.

Footsteps echo, soft and low,
A fleeting touch, a ghostly glow.
Figures blend with fading light,
Lurking still, they haunt the night.

Curved reflections, shapes of dread,
In corners where the fears are fed.
Glimmers of what might have been,
Caught in the half-light, lost between.

Murmurs weave through tangled trees,
A melody on the breeze.
In this realm where dreams take flight,
Lurking deep within the night.

Shadows of the Heart

Underneath the silver moon,
Life's secrets sing a soft tune.
Whispers swirl like autumn leaves,
Traces left of what deceives.

In the silence, feelings stir,
Shadows flicker, hearts confer.
Moments passed but never lost,
Echoes linger, count the cost.

Distant stars watch from afar,
Guiding light, a hope-filled scar.
In the depths where fears reside,
Shadows of the heart confide.

Wrapped in velvet silence deep,
Promises that time must keep.
In the night, the truth takes flight,
Shadows whisper, wrong or right.

The Language of Silence

Words unspoken, heavy air,
Eyes that meet, a silent stare.
In the quiet, feelings swell,
The language of silence tells.

Gentle sighs, a tender glance,
In this stillness, hearts advance.
Between the lines, a story brews,
In the hush, the soul renews.

Fingers brush, a fleeting spark,
Soft as shadows in the dark.
Each heartbeat, a phrase of grace,
The silent bond, our secret space.

Unraveled thoughts without a sound,
In this calm, love's pulse is found.
In the echo, life aligns,
The language of silence shines.

Ghosts of Last Night

Memories drift like restless shades,
Whispers haunt in twilight glades.
Footsteps linger, soft and near,
Ghosts of last night, vivid and clear.

In the corners of the mind,
Echoes of what we left behind.
Haunting laughs and subtle sighs,
Fleeting dreams weave through the skies.

Through the veil of sleep, they roam,
Searching for a place called home.
In our thoughts, they won't depart,
Ghosts of last night reside in heart.

In the morning light, they fade,
But their essence will not trade.
For in our dreams, they come alive,
Ghosts of last night, forever thrive.

Whispers of the Dark

In shadows deep the secrets dwell,
Forgotten dreams weave tales to tell.
Stars flicker dim, a silent shout,
While night unveils what we live without.

The moonlight dances on paths untread,
As whispers weave through the hearts we dread.
The silence speaks in haunting tones,
Reminding us we're not alone.

Ghostly figures in the mist do wane,
Echoing soft the joy and pain.
Each pulse of night, a tender sigh,
Hiding truths in the fabric of why.

So linger here, let darkness flow,
For in the dark, there's much to know.
Each secret shared within the night,
Illuminates what's lost from sight.

Veils of Unspoken Truth

Beneath the silence, whispers hide,
Secrets wrapped in a fragile tide.
Veils of thoughts that drift and weave,
Stopping hearts from what they believe.

Concealed behind a knowing glance,
The weight of things left to chance.
In quiet breaths, the world stands still,
On the edge of hope, we dare to feel.

Layers unfold like petals shy,
In gardens where our sorrows lie.
Words unsaid carve paths of pain,
Yet promise blooms with love's refrain.

So speak the truths you fear to name,
In light of day, there's no more shame.
For in the open, hearts can mend,
And veils of truth will find their end.

Beneath the Gloom

Beneath the gloom, shadows stretch wide,
Where dreams are lost and hopes divide.
A heavy fog, we wander through,
Searching for light, for something new.

Cold winds whisper of days gone by,
As echoes of laughter seem to sigh.
In the silence, we grasp for dawn,
Yearning for warmth before it's gone.

Footsteps linger on paths of sorrow,
Hopes entwined with a distant morrow.
Yet in the depths, a flicker stirs,
A spark of joy that still occurs.

So rise from shadows, let courage bloom,
For bright tomorrows can mend the gloom.
In every heart, a fire waits,
To blaze through dark and open gates.

Echoes of Hidden Realms

In realms unseen, where echoes call,
Veiled whispers drift, do softly fall.
An unseen world, where dreams converge,
With every heartbeat, secrets surge.

Through thickets dense, the pathways wind,
Where truth and fantasy intertwine.
The echoes hum of tales untold,
In golden hues and threads of old.

Each step we take, a bridge to find,
The hidden depths of heart and mind.
With every sigh, the past ignites,
Unraveling the silent nights.

So listen close, let silence hum,
For in those depths, new worlds will come.
With open hearts, we dare to roam,
In echoes sweet, we find our home.

The Mask We Wear

In crowded rooms we hide our face,
A smile placed with careful grace.
Beneath the laughter, shadows loom,
A heart encased, a spirit's gloom.

We weave our tales with threads so fine,
In daylight's glow, the truth declines.
Each mask we wear, a fragile shield,
Our secrets kept, our wounds concealed.

Yet in the night, when darkness calls,
The mask may slip, the silence falls.
In shadows deep, we find our core,
And let the spirits rise and soar.

So dare to cast those masks away,
Embrace the truth in bright array.
For underneath, we're all the same,
In love and light, we stake our claim.

In the Depths of Dusk

As sun descends, the world turns gray,
Whispers float, dusk leads the sway.
Colors bleed into the night,
Stars awaken, a guiding light.

The shadows stir, they softly creep,
Secrets dwell where silence sleeps.
Beneath the sky, dreams start to bloom,
In twilight's hush, we find our room.

The air is thick with stories untold,
Embers glow, turning warm and bold.
In the depths where darkness stirs,
Magic brews and softly blurs.

In stillness wrapped, we breathe so slow,
The heartbeats echo, gently flow.
In the dusk, we find our way,
Where night and hopes begin to play.

Cloaks of Mystery

With every glance, a story waits,
Wrapped in silence, it resonates.
Cloaks of mystery, draped with care,
In shadows woven, secrets share.

Through veils of thought, we drift along,
Listening closely to the unspoken song.
Eyes revealing what lips won't dare,
In the quiet moments, truth laid bare.

Embrace the enigma, the unknown path,
Where curiosity invites its wrath.
Beneath the layers, we all reside,
Unlocking doors, casting fear aside.

So wear your cloak with pride and grace,
In this ballet, find your place.
For every mystery calls your name,
And in its depths, we're all the same.

When Silence Speaks

In spaces where the echoes play,
Whispers echo what hearts can't say.
The stillness hums a gentle tune,
Beneath the stars, under the moon.

In quiet corners, truths unfold,
A language formed, yet never told.
In every pause, the heart can leap,
For sweetness lies when silence speaks.

The absence of sound can fill the air,
With emotions rich, a tender flare.
Unraveled thoughts begin to bloom,
In the hush of night, we find our room.

So listen close when silence sighs,
For in its depth, true magic lies.
With every heartbeat, hear the plea,
That silence speaks, setting us free.

Beneath the Gaze of the Moon

Whispers dance in silver light,
Dreams awaken in the night.
Stars above begin to gleam,
Cradling every whispered dream.

Cascading shadows, soft and slight,
Guide hearts lost in endless flight.
Underneath this cosmic dome,
We find magic in the unknown.

The cool breeze carries ancient tales,
While nightingale softly hails.
A world transformed in lunar glow,
Where secrets flourish, and love can flow.

Embrace the quiet, let it seep,
Profound moments lull us to sleep.
Beneath the gaze, a tender balm,
In moonlit stillness, we find calm.

Twilight's Hidden Truths

In the twilight's gentle sigh,
The world shifts, and shadows lie.
Colors blend, a masterpiece,
As day retreats, and echoes cease.

Secrets hide in dusky tones,
Where silence whispers, truth atones.
Fleeting moments, veils of time,
In twilight's grasp, all feels sublime.

Stars begin their nightly chase,
Each twinkle, an embrace of grace.
Among the dusk, we wander free,
In twilight's arms, we cease to be.

As night descends, our fears take flight,
Revealing dreams concealed by light.
In hidden truths, we'll find our way,
Guided softly by the fray.

Shadows of the Unexplored

In the depths where shadows blend,
Curiosity finds its end.
A realm where whispers roam anew,
And mysteries await the view.

Paths untraveled hold their breath,
Echoes of life, a dance with death.
Footsteps linger, pause, and stare,
In hushed moments, time lays bare.

Branches stretch as secrets ache,
Beneath the leaves, the lost forsake.
With every rustle, stories glide,
In shadows deep, we learn to hide.

Embrace the dark, let wonder reign,
In unexplored, we break the chain.
A tapestry of dusk unfolds,
Where unseen wonders call the bold.

Echoes of the Unseen

In the silence, echoes dwell,
Faint reminders, tales to tell.
Unseen moments linger here,
A soft whisper, a hushed cheer.

Through the veil of time we tread,
Footprints linger, lost and spread.
In every pause, a heartbeat waits,
Revelations sealed by fate.

Glimmers fade in autumn's breath,
Life and death weave threads of depth.
In shadows cast, the truth will gleam,
An unseen world, a living dream.

Listen closely, hear the call,
Embrace the rise, surrender fall.
In echoes, wisdom waits for thee,
A world beyond what eyes can see.

The Soft Touch of Oblivion

In twilight's hush, dreams softly fade,
A gentle mist, serenely laid.
With every sigh, the past unwinds,
In shadows deep, the silence binds.

Forgotten paths, where whispers dwell,
In echoes lost, our secrets swell.
The heart recalls what time forgot,
In sweet embrace, we linger, caught.

A feather's grace, a fleeting thought,
In stillness found, yet always sought.
We drift like leaves on rivers wide,
In soft oblivion, we confide.

The moonlight glows, a silent thief,
Stealing moments, granting brief relief.
In fading light, we find our peace,
As soft oblivion grants release.

Whispers of Concealed Truths

In shadows sharp, the truth does hide,
Amongst the lies, we often bide.
Each hidden thought, a delicate thread,
Woven in silence, always misread.

Beneath the smiles, a knowing glance,
Unraveled secrets in a fleeting dance.
With hearts entwined, the whispers grow,
In quiet corners, the secrets flow.

The air is thick with unspoken words,
While hidden hopes take flight like birds.
A fragile trust, a whispered sound,
In this stillness, truths abound.

In veils of night, our spirits yearn,
For each concealed truth, there's always a turn.
As dreams disperse, we seek the light,
To find the truths that hide from sight.

The Subtle Breath of Night

In velvet skies, the night unfurls,
With whispered secrets, softly swirls.
The moon, a guardian, watches near,
Guiding lost souls, calming fear.

Beneath the stars, the world holds breath,
As silence dances, teasing death.
In this embrace, we find our calm,
In night's sweet breath, a healing balm.

The shadows play on ancient walls,
Where memories linger, softly calls.
With every heartbeat, time stands still,
As night unfolds its gentle will.

A world reborn in dusky shades,
Where dreams ignite and fear cascades.
In twilight's grip, we learn to trust,
The subtle breath of night is just.

Mystic Underworlds

In whispered realms where echoes dwell,
Lies a hidden world, a cryptic spell.
Through veils of time, in depths we roam,
Our hearts entwined in the unknown.

The rivers flow with shadows deep,
Where ancient secrets dare not sleep.
In caves adorned with stories old,
Our souls seek truths that long have told.

With spirits bright, we venture forth,
To find the keys that unlock worth.
In mystic underworlds, we glide,
With every breath, our fears subside.

A labyrinth of dreams and fate,
Where every path leads to create.
In hidden places, we discover,
The mystic bond that draws us closer.

The Color of Shadows

Shadows whisper in the night,
Painting dreams in muted light.
Colors blend in twilight's grace,
Mysteries haunt this hidden space.

Beneath the boughs of ancient trees,
Secrets rustle in the breeze.
If you listen, you might hear,
Echoes of what's close and near.

Figures dance without a face,
In this realm, time leaves no trace.
Fingers stretch to touch the void,
In this stillness, souls get buoyed.

Awake, aware, the shadows loom,
Painting futures from the gloom.
Each corner holds a tale untold,
In the color of shadows bold.

Enigmas in the Gloaming

Gloaming wraps the world in gray,
Where the night begins to play.
Softly fading, day retreats,
Whispers dance on twilight streets.

Every glance, a fleeting spark,
Hides a truth waiting in the dark.
Enigmas cloaked in misty shrouds,
Beneath the gaze of curling clouds.

Footsteps echo, just a trace,
Leading to a hidden place.
Questions swirl like autumn leaves,
In the hush that softly weaves.

Secrets lift on evening's sigh,
While the stars begin to cry.
Gloaming's magic, ever close,
Invites us to explore, engrossed.

Threads of the Hidden

Woven tight, the threads remain,
Holding stories, joy and pain.
Colors shimmer in the night,
Beneath the veil of silent light.

Each strand speaks of paths once crossed,
Of dreams fulfilled and visions lost.
Tangled in the fabric fine,
Life's design, a fragile line.

In the shadows, whispers weave,
Intertwined, we come to believe.
Binding hearts with tender care,
Threads of fate weave everywhere.

Unseen hands, a guiding touch,
Revealing truths that mean so much.
Embrace the fibers, dark and bright,
In the threads of the hidden night.

Hallow's Mysterious Embrace

In the glow of autumn's breath,
Hallow's night stirs thoughts of death.
Candles flicker, shadows play,
As the warmth begins to sway.

Ghostly whispers wrap the air,
Secrets float in evening's glare.
Figures move in silent grace,
From beyond, they leave no trace.

Cloaked in veil, the moments pause,
Captured in a world of cause.
Every shadow holds a spark,
In Hallow's embrace, it's never dark.

Hold your breath and take a chance,
Join the spirits in their dance.
In the night where dreams awake,
Hallow's magic, souls partake.

Enigmatic Whispers

In shadows deep, secrets intertwine,
The night air hums, a cryptic sign.
Soft murmurs echo through the trees,
Where every breeze carries mysteries.

Veils of silence cloak the truth,
Ancient tales, the wisdom of youth.
Stars above glimmer, faint but bright,
Guiding lost souls in the still of night.

Every glance hides a tale untold,
Layers unfold, as moments unfold.
Eyes speak volumes, hearts softly yearn,
For the secrets that time will return.

In twilight's grasp, we seek, we find,
The whispers of fate, entwined and blind.
Close your eyes, let the magic flow,
In enigmatic whispers, truth will grow.

Silent Confessions

Beneath the surface, feelings reside,
Soft words linger, where dreams abide.
A heart exposed, yet guarded so tight,
In silent confessions, love takes flight.

The weight of silence, heavy and grand,
Between the moments, we take our stand.
A shared glance speaks louder than roars,
In the quiet, our spirit soars.

Each heartbeat whispers, tales of the soul,
Fragmented truths making us whole.
In the stillness, vulnerabilities sway,
Silent confessions, come what may.

Through whispers of night, our secrets entwine,
In shadows, we find a love so divine.
Let the world fade, just you and I,
In these silent confessions, we learn to fly.

Mysteries Beneath the Surface

Ripples dance on a calm, deep lake,
Beneath the surface, dreams awake.
What lies hidden, beyond the sight?
Mysteries wrapped in the cloak of night.

Tales of the past, in waters conceal,
Whispers of values we long to feel.
With each wave's crash, answers will blend,
In depths unknown, truths never end.

The cool touch of the water's embrace,
In its depths, we seek solace and grace.
Each echo calls, a timeless refrain,
Mysteries beneath that cannot contain.

When twilight descends, our hearts align,
Entranced by the secrets the waters define.
In this stillness, we learn and dive,
To uncover the mysteries where dreams survive.

Unseen Corners of the Night

In twilight's grip, where shadows creep,
Unseen corners hold secrets to keep.
Starlight flickers, illuminating the dark,
Every hidden space, a waiting spark.

Whispers linger in the hallowed air,
A haunting melody, sweet despair.
Through the alleys, forgotten stories flow,
Unseen corners whisper what we may know.

Dreams take flight in the silence of night,
Where hidden hopes ignite with delight.
In every hush, a heartbeat's call,
Unseen corners cradle us all.

Beneath the moon's watchful, tender gaze,
We wander through life's intricate maze.
In the mystery lies the beauty of flight,
In unseen corners, we find our light.

Cloaked in Dusk

Shadows stretch as day fades away,
Whispers of night begin their play.
Colors blend in twilight's embrace,
A gentle sigh fills the empty space.

Stars twinkle like secrets untold,
The world wraps in a blanket of gold.
The moon rises, a watchful eye,
Guarding dreams as they float and fly.

In this hour, time slows its chase,
Each moment savored, none left to waste.
Nature breathes, in harmony's tune,
Cloaked in the mystery of the moon.

In shadows deep, our thoughts ignite,
Cloaked in the magic of coming night.
Beneath the stars, our spirits roam,
In dusky hours, we find our home.

The Language of Silence

Between the hearts lies a quiet place,
Where words dissolve without a trace.
In glances shared, emotions bloom,
A soft embrace dispels the gloom.

Silence speaks with a gentle hand,
It bridges worlds, makes us understand.
In the calm, we hear the truth,
The voice of wisdom, the song of youth.

Listen closely to the stillness there,
Every heartbeat, a silent prayer.
The language cherished, not often heard,
In the hush, we find our world.

In moments brief, connections grow,
A powerful bond, unseen but known.
Together we linger, softly we stand,
In the realm of silence, hand in hand.

Phantoms of Forgotten Dreams

In twilight's mist, memories drift,
Phantoms linger, a haunting gift.
Echoes of laughter, whispers of tears,
Lost in the shadows, held by our fears.

Dreams once vibrant, now faint glows,
In dusty corners, the past bestows.
Each flicker a tale, woven in thread,
Of hopes unfulfilled, but never dead.

Through the silence, we seek their call,
Fleeting apparitions, we recall.
Yet in their presence, there lies a spark,
Guiding us gently through the dark.

In the heart's chambers, they softly wade,
Phantoms remain, never to fade.
Awake in the night, we cherish their flight,
In dreams forgotten, they bring us light.

In the Stillness, They Speak

In quiet moments, truth takes flight,
Softly spoken, in the dimest light.
Nature pauses, breaths align,
In the stillness, wisdom divine.

The rustling leaves, a secret song,
In tranquil tones, where we belong.
Stars whisper truths in cosmic sighs,
In the silent space, our spirits rise.

The heart listens to every plea,
In the stillness, we find the key.
To unlock the depths of our soul's array,
In the silence, they guide our way.

So linger here, embrace the calm,
In the stillness, there's a healing balm.
Let harmony cradle the weary heart,
In silence, a brand new start.

Hushed Vows in the Dark

In shadows deep, whispers flow,
Secrets shared, where no light goes.
Promises made, hearts entwined,
In the dark, true love we find.

Silent gazes, tender grace,
Holding dreams in a sacred space.
With every sigh, a pledge is heard,
In the silence, love's own word.

Time stands still, the world fades away,
In this moment, forever we'll stay.
Stars witness our vows, serene and bright,
Guiding us softly through the night.

Together we stand, against all fears,
In the hush of night, we shed our tears.
For in the dark, our spirits soar,
Hushed vows whispered, forevermore.

The Linger of Ghostlights

In twilight's glow, they softly gleam,
Fading echoes of a forgotten dream.
Whispers drift on a spectral breeze,
Ghostlights dance among the trees.

Flickering softly, teasing the dark,
A fleeting glimpse of life's old spark.
Lost in shadows, they glide and sway,
Drawing memories that never decay.

They weave through time, elusive and light,
Guiding lost souls in the still of night.
A silent beckoning, gentle and clear,
The linger of ghostlights, always near.

In the hush of dusk, secrets remain,
The dance of the past, an ethereal chain.
With each flicker, our hearts recall,
The stories of love that outlast it all.

Veils of Enigma

Wrapped in mystery, time unfolds,
Veils of enigma, secrets untold.
Whispers of night in shadows we weave,
Unraveling stories that hearts believe.

Soft as a sigh, the echoes abide,
Hidden in layers, where thoughts reside.
A labyrinth rich with paths unknown,
In every shadow, a truth has grown.

Among the thorns, blossoms arise,
Truths revealed in the stillest skies.
Entangled fates, we wander and roam,
Through veils of enigma, we seek our home.

Glimmers of light tease the dark away,
In the dance of fate, we learn to sway.
Each step a question, each turn a chance,
To uncover the meaning in life's grand dance.

Shrouded in Silence

Veiled in quiet, the world holds its breath,
In the stillness lies a promise of breadth.
Each whispered thought, a delicate thread,
Woven together, where love is bred.

Amidst the hush, hearts gently align,
A sacred bond, through space and time.
Silenced laughter, joy set free,
In the canvas of quiet, we find the key.

The moonlight drapes a shroud so fine,
Encasing dreams in a soft design.
With every heartbeat, a rhythm profound,
In silence, our destinies are found.

Held in the gentle clasp of night,
Shrouded in silence, our spirits take flight.
For in the calm, our love will grow,
In hushes and whispers, our hearts will know.

Beneath the Surface

Whispers dance in liquid dark,
Ripples trace the hidden arc.
Depths conceal a world so vast,
Silent secrets hold their cast.

Bubbles rise like fleeting dreams,
Softly breaking at the seams.
Creatures glint with stories old,
In shadows deep, their truths unfold.

A current pulls, a tide's embrace,
Drawing forth a secret place.
Where visions blend with light and gloom,
Beneath the waves, life finds its room.

Candles flicker, shadows weave,
In the depths, we dare believe.
What lies hidden, not to surf,
Awakens softly—beneath the surf.

They Lurk

In the corners, shadows creep,
While the weary find their sleep.
Figures break the beams of light,
Murmurs echo through the night.

Eyes that glint with secret fire,
Hearts entwined in whispered choir.
What they know remains unsaid,
Haunting paths where few have tread.

Silhouettes on midnight's stage,
Puzzles locked within a cage.
Every footstep, every breath,
Woven threads of life and death.

When the silence draws its veil,
Their presence tells an ancient tale.
In that stillness, they remain,
Guardians of a shadowed reign.

The Night's Secret Symphony

Moonlight bathes the world in glow,
Softly turning dreams to show.
Stars compose their nightly score,
Each note whispers, asking for more.

Gentle breezes weave through trees,
Carrying the song of leaves.
Crickets chirp a tender tune,
As shadows dance beneath the moon.

Night's embrace holds stories dear,
Echoes of what we hold near.
With each moment, magic swells,
In the night, a world compels.

Listen close, let silence reign,
In the dark, find joy and pain.
Harmony in twilight's art,
The secret symphony's sweet heart.

Elusive Forms in the Twilight

Shapes emerging from the night,
Flitting figures out of sight.
Hints of color, whispers low,
In twilight's grip, they softly flow.

Veils of mist weave through the trees,
Catching shadows in the breeze.
Fleeting forms that slip away,
In the dusk, they come to play.

Unseen dancers on the ground,
Echoes of a silent sound.
In the gloam, their echoes tease,
A tapestry of mysteries.

Every glance begins a chase,
Forms that vanish without trace.
Elusive spirits, lost yet near,
In twilight's dance, we hold them dear.

A Tapestry of Shadows

Threads of dusk and dawning grey,
Stitch the night and blend the day.
Every shadow tells a tale,
In the silence where dreams sail.

Canvas wide, the world unfolds,
Patterns woven, stories told.
Flickers, pools of dark and light,
Creating worlds in gentle flight.

Whispers linger in the air,
Embroidered moments, rich and rare.
Beneath the surface, life takes form,
A tapestry where dreams are born.

In every shade, a life anew,
Colors blend where visions grew.
Embrace the shadows, let them sway,
A tapestry of night and day.

Chasing Reflections

In the mirror, shadows play,
Whispers of the life we sway,
Every glance a fleeting chance,
Moments lost in a silent dance.

Eyes that sparkle, hearts uninhibited,
Dreams unfold, our hopes exhibited,
Yet, in the glass, truth hides away,
Chasing reflections, night and day.

Fleeting glimpses in twilight's hue,
Searching for a piece of you,
Echoes echoing through the air,
A haunting memory, a gentle dare.

Through corridors of time, we roam,
Wandering paths, far from home,
In each reflection, we find the light,
Chasing shadows into the night.

The Other Side of Midnight

The clock ticks softly, whispers low,
Secrets hidden in the glow,
Of stars that twinkle, dreams take flight,
On the other side of midnight's plight.

Time stands still, a breath in pause,
Moments woven without a cause,
In this quiet, surreal expanse,
We find a rhythm, we begin to dance.

Silhouettes blend in the dark,
While shadows linger, they leave a mark,
Delicate whispers on the breeze,
A haunting song that aims to please.

Through the hours that gently blur,
Every heartbeat begins to stir,
On the edge of dreams and fears,
The other side calls, as silence nears.

At the Edge of Oblivion

Where the light dims, the silence reigns,
Echoes tumble through forgotten lanes,
At the edge where shadows creep,
Lies a truth we seldom keep.

Whispers beckon from deep within,
Fragments of world where we've been,
In twilight's grasp, the dawn is thin,
At the edge where dreams begin.

By the river of lost refrains,
We linger on, through joy and pains,
Each breath a battle, each step a fight,
At the edge of the endless night.

Yet in the darkness, a spark does glow,
A reminder of warmth we used to know,
At the edge of oblivion, hope will gleam,
A flicker of light, a distant dream.

Murmurs in the Dimness

In the hush of twilight's embrace,
Murmurs linger without a trace,
Soft as the breeze that carries night,
Fleeting whispers, lost in flight.

The moon hangs low, a watchful eye,
Casting secrets as moments fly,
In shadowed corners, stories weave,
Murmurs in dimness, we believe.

Every sigh, a silent prayer,
A longing echo in the air,
In the stillness, our hearts align,
Murmurs of love and the divine.

Through the depths, we softly tread,
On paths of dreams and words unsaid,
In dimness, together we find,
Murmurs of solace, gently intertwined.

The Unseen Veil

Behind the curtain, shadows play,
Secrets linger, hidden sway,
A whisper calls, yet remains still,
Softly draped in silence's thrill.

Glimmers of truth, masked by night,
Hidden stories, out of sight,
The heart beats loud, yet muted too,
In every breath, the unseen view.

Veils of dreams softly spun,
Cloaked in dusk, when day is done,
Fingers trace the hidden lore,
In the stillness, we seek more.

As dawn breaks and light unfolds,
The secrets shared, once untold,
The veil lifts, revealing all,
In soft hues, we heed the call.

Night's Hushed Confessions

In the dark, where whispers blend,
Secrets flow, they twist and bend,
Stars above hold stories wide,
Night's embrace, where dreams reside.

Each sigh carries tales untold,
In velvet shades, the night is bold,
Hushed confessions, softly shared,
In the quiet, hearts stripped bare.

Moonlit paths guide wandering souls,
Flickering lanterns, gentle goals,
Together bound, we steal the night,
In shadows cast, we find the light.

As dawn creeps in, the tales dissolve,
In morning's glow, we will resolve,
Yet night shall keep its secrets tight,
In whispers lost, beneath our sight.

Shrouded Reveries

Beneath the mist, they softly weave,
Shrouded dreams that hearts believe,
In gentle folds, the past retreats,
Silent echoes, where memory meets.

Veiled in fog, the dawn awaits,
Time stands still, as fate debates,
Twilight dances, shadows blend,
In reveries, we find our friend.

Whispers linger, soft and clear,
Threads of hope, intertwined near,
A tapestry of light and shade,
In shrouded halls, our fears allayed.

As night concedes to morning's grace,
The dreams take flight, they leave their trace,
In every tremor, we believe,
In shrouded days, we dare to dream.

Fables of the Forgotten

Once there lived tales in the breeze,
Woven words in ancient trees,
Echoes call from realms afar,
Fables lost, like shooting stars.

Pages turned, but stories fade,
In shadowed woods, the paths we laid,
Every heart bears ancient scars,
Underneath the watching stars.

Memory lingers, softly calls,
In the quiet, the silence falls,
Forgotten legends whisper low,
In the dark, their truths still glow.

Yet with each dusk, a spark ignites,
In the dark, old fables light,
We gather round, and there we'll find,
The timeless tales that bind mankind.

Unraveled Under Starlight

Beneath the vast and velvet sky,
Dreams whisper softly, hopes fly high.
Stars awaken tales of old,
In the night, their secrets unfold.

The moon's embrace, a gentle guide,
Where shadows linger, fears subside.
Unraveled threads of light and dark,
Illuminate the hidden spark.

Each twinkle whispers, tales anew,
Of paths we walked and skies so blue.
In the stillness, hearts align,
Unraveled dreams in pure design.

Lost in wonder, we shall roam,
Under starlight, we find our home.
In every flicker, stories blend,
Where beginnings and endings mend.

Shadows Dance in Silence

In the corners where the light fades,
Shadows twirl in hidden glades.
Movements soft as whispered sighs,
In silence, the darkness lies.

Echoes linger in muted halls,
Where whispered secrets softly call.
Each edge blurs, each form bends,
In this quiet, time transcends.

Glimmers haunt the midnight air,
Fleeting whispers, none to share.
In the stillness, a story lives,
A dance of silence that forgives.

Shadows weave a tale of lore,
Of hearts that loved and yearned for more.
In the twilight, a truth enchants,
As shadows dance, the silence grants.

Tales Untold

In every heart, a story dwells,
Of whispered dreams and ringing bells.
Tales untold in a silent cry,
Yearning to reach the endless sky.

The ink of night spills words unspoken,
Promises made, and hearts left broken.
Every glance, a chapter penned,
In the book of time, we shall bend.

A gentle breath, a fleeting glance,
Underneath the stars, we dance.
Between the lines, life intertwines,
In every shadow, hope brightly shines.

Tales await, as dreams unfold,
In the corners where secrets hold.
With every heartbeat, a truth retold,
In the silence, tales yet bold.

Furtive Gleams of Light

In quiet corners, shadows creep,
Yet furtive gleams, they softly seep.
A dance of hope in dim-lit rooms,
Where every flicker gently blooms.

Beneath the hush of veiled nights,
Small sparks ignite as whispers fly.
The heart, it skips with each new spark,
As light pierces through the stark.

Moments cherished, fleeting bright,
Hidden gems in shrouded sight.
With every gleam, a promise grows,
In tender luminescence, it glows.

Amidst the shadows, we discover,
The light within, like no other.
Furtive gleams that guide our way,
Illuminate the dawning day.

Milton Keynes UK
Ingram Content Group UK Ltd.
UKHW021128021124
450571UK00005B/75